EXPLORING COUNTRIES

China

by Walter Simmons

BELLWETHER MEDIA · MINNEAPOLIS, MN

Note to Librarians, Teachers, and Parents:

Blastoff! Readers are carefully developed by literacy experts and combine standards-based content with developmentally appropriate text.

Level 1 provides the most support through repetition of high-frequency words, light text, predictable sentence patterns, and strong visual support.

Level 2 offers early readers a bit more challenge through varied simple sentences, increased text load, and less repetition of high-frequency words.

Level 3 advances early-fluent readers toward fluency through increased text and concept load, less reliance on visuals, longer sentences, and more literary language.

Level 4 builds reading stamina by providing more text per page, increased use of punctuation, greater variation in sentence patterns, and increasingly challenging vocabulary.

Level 5 encourages children to move from "learning to read" to "reading to learn" by providing even more text, varied writing styles, and less familiar topics.

Whichever book is right for your reader, Blastoff! Readers are the perfect books to build confidence and encourage a love of reading that will last a lifetime!

This edition first published in 2011 by Bellwether Media, Inc.

No part of this publication may be reproduced in whole or in part without written permission of the publisher. For information regarding permission, write to Bellwether Media, Inc., Attention: Permissions Department, 5357 Penn Avenue South, Minneapolis, MN 55419.

Library of Congress Cataloging-in-Publication Data

Simmons, Walter (Walter G.)
China / by Walter Simmons.
    p. cm. – (Blastoff! readers: Exploring countries)
Includes bibliographical references and index.
Summary: "Developed by literacy experts for students in grades three through seven, this book introduces young readers to the geography and culture of China"–Provided by publisher.
ISBN 978-1-60014-476-9 (hardcover : alk. paper)
1. China–Juvenile literature. I. Title.
DS706.S4877 2010
951–dc22   2010009209

Printed in the United States of America, North Mankato, MN.

080110   1162

Contents

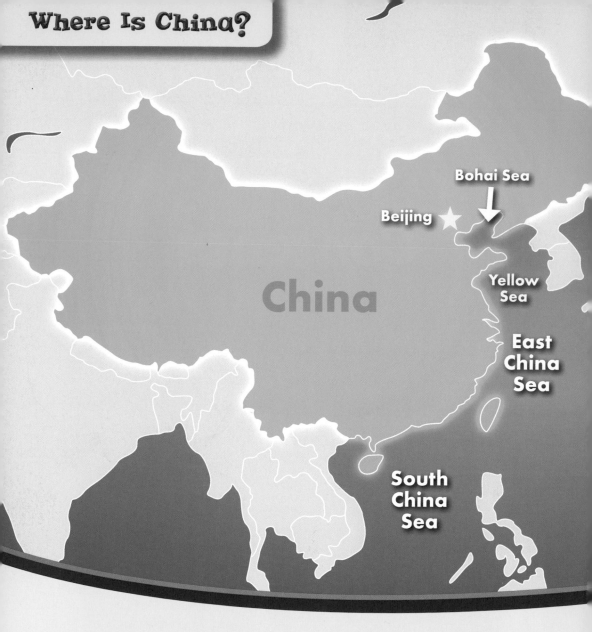

China is a large nation that spans much of Southeast Asia. With an area of 3,705,407 square miles (9,596,961 square kilometers), it is the fourth-largest country in the world. Only Russia, Canada, and the United States are larger. The capital of China is Beijing.

fun fact

China was founded almost 1,800 years ago. It is one of the oldest countries in the world!

China borders countries in southeastern, northern, and central Asia. In total, it has fourteen neighbors. It also borders four seas. Northeastern China touches the Yellow Sea and the Bohai Sea. The East China Sea and the South China Sea lie along China's southeastern coast.

China has many different landscapes. In the deserts of northwestern China, many people travel on camelback. The dry Gobi Desert, where few people live, separates China and Mongolia. Farmers grow crops on the **fertile** green hills and grasslands that cover much of the south and east. Mountains rise in the western, northern, and southern parts of China.

Two major rivers wind through China. Both rivers flow from west to east. The sands of the Gobi Desert color the Yellow River, which runs through northern China. The Yangtze, the major river of the south, rushes through steep valleys and mountain gorges.

! fun fact

Thousands of dinosaur fossils have been found in and around the city of Dashanpu. The fossils are estimated to be over 100 million years old!

Did you know?
The Yangtze flows for 3,915 miles (6,300 kilometers), making it the longest river in Asia.

Tibet is a high **plateau** in southwestern China that borders the Himalayan Mountains. It is one of the highest plateaus on Earth and is often called the "Roof of the World." Tibet's average height is over 13,125 feet (4,000 meters). The air is thin and very dry in Tibet. In winter, cold winds blow down from the mountain peaks.

Mount Everest, part of the Himalayas, towers over southern Tibet. The people of Tibet call this mountain *Qomolangma*. With a height of 29,035 feet (8,850 meters), it is the world's highest peak. The mountain is very dangerous for climbers. Its slopes are slippery and steep.

Potala Palace

fun fact

The massive Potala Palace is located in Tibet. It has over 1,000 rooms, 10,000 shrines, and 200,000 statues!

Mount Everest

giant panda

fun fact

A giant panda often eats more than 40 pounds (18 kilograms) of bamboo in one day!

Animals thrive in the wild places of China. In the forests, giant pandas enjoy meals of **bamboo**. Red pandas **forage** for food on the ground and in the trees. The rare Siberian tiger and South China tiger hunt wild deer and antelope. China's mountains are home to snow leopards, wolves, and foxes. The golden pheasant lives in the forests and mountains of western China.

golden pheasant

snow leopard

red panda

In the northwestern deserts live Bactrian camels. These camels have two humps. Other desert animals include musk oxen, eagles, lizards, and the **endangered** Gobi bear. The waters in and around China are full of life. Alligators and water deer live along China's rivers. The rivers are home to carp and paddlefish. Dugongs, seals, and sharks swim off the Chinese coasts.

11

China is home to about 1.3 billion people. More people live in China than in any other country. Several different ethnic groups live in China. The Han live throughout the nation and make up the biggest group. Nine out of ten Chinese people are Han. Koreans and Mongolians live in northern China, while southern China is home to the Yao and the Miao.

fun fact

The people of the Long Horn Miao tribe are known for the fancy hairstyles they wear on special occasions. They add linen, wool, and hair from their ancestors to their own hair.

Speak Mandarin!

Mandarin is written in characters.
However, Mandarin words can be written in
English to help you read them out loud.

English	Mandarin	How to say it
hello	ni hao	nee how
good-bye	zai jian	za-ee jee-an
yes	shi	shr
no	bu shi	boo shr
please	qing	ching
thank you	xie-xie	shee-eh-shee-eh
friend	peng-you	peng-yo

Did you know?

Mandarin is one of six official languages of the United Nations. The other five are Arabic, English, French, Russian, and Spanish.

Most Chinese people speak Mandarin, but there are many other languages. Xiang, Cantonese, and Min are also spoken in China. People in the city of Shanghai speak a language called Wu. When they speak to outsiders, they use Mandarin or English.

Life in China is different for people in the city and those in
the countryside. People in cities live in small apartments.
They use buses, trains, and bicycles to get around.
Today, some families who live in cities are buying cars for
the first time. The workday ends in the late afternoon.
Families gather for dinner and relax at home. Many people
like to go outside for a walk or to visit their neighbors.

Where People Live in China

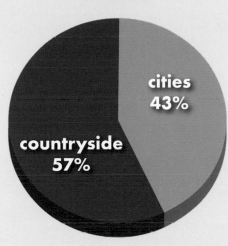

cities 43%

countryside 57%

In the countryside, farmers live in villages where the homes are made of brick or stone. People draw water from wells outside their homes and cook inside over open fires. They travel to larger cities by car or train to shop for goods they cannot find in their villages.

Did you know?

In many villages, women do the hard work of planting and harvesting crops. Their husbands and sons often go to the cities to find work.

15

Going to School

Most children in China start school when they are 6 years old. Elementary school usually lasts six years. Middle school often takes three years, and high school three more. Everyone must go to school for at least nine years. Students learn math, science, Mandarin, art, physical education, and other subjects. English and other foreign languages are introduced to students around third grade.

fun fact

The Chinese write in characters. Each character stands for a word or a sound. Mandarin is thought to have around 50,000 characters. The average Chinese person knows a few thousand.

If students finish high school, they can start working or go to a school that gives them training for a specific job. If they want to go to a university, they have to pass a tough exam. The number of students in China who attend university has increased in recent years.

Where People Work in China

farming 39.5%

manufacturing 27.3%

services 33.2%

Many Chinese people work in factories in big cities. Some factory workers make toys, shoes, clothes, and electronics. Others build ships, trains, airplanes, and cars. Construction workers are helping China's cities grow. They build roads, buildings, and skyscrapers. Many Chinese people have **service jobs**. They work in banks, restaurants, and other businesses.

Farming and mining are big industries in the countryside. Farmers raise chickens, pigs, and other livestock. They also grow rice, wheat, peanuts, and tea. Miners dig up coal, copper, and other **natural resources** from the earth.

Did you know?
At the Shaolin Monastery, monks have practiced the martial art of Shaolin *kung fu* for hundreds of years.

The Chinese spend their free time doing many activities. Millions of people watch and play basketball, soccer, and volleyball. The Chinese also love ping-pong and **badminton**. Ping-pong tables are often set up in streets and parks. Many Chinese people exercise every day. Some practice **martial arts** such as *karate* and *kung fu*. In *tai chi*, people slowly move through a series of poses and carefully balance their bodies.

The Chinese also enjoy shopping in malls, watching TV, or going to movies. Chinese families often travel. They can go camping or hiking in any of China's 208 national parks.

! fun fact

At the 2008 Summer Olympics, China won eight medals in ping-pong.

Did you know?
Cantonese food is traditionally cooked in southern China but is famous throughout the world.

Chinese food uses a wide range of meats, fish, vegetables, and **herbs**. Cooks also use spicy peppers, and rice appears with almost every meal. When rice is fried with vegetables, eggs, and other ingredients, it is called fried rice. **Dumplings** are also popular throughout China. Some dumplings, like *wontons*, are used in soups.

Only cooks cut and chop food in China. According to tradition, there are no knives at the dining table. The Chinese eat with spoons and **chopsticks**. The dishes all sit in the center of the table. People choose what they want and bring it to their plate or bowl.

fun fact

In China, noodles made with peanut oil and garlic are said to bring long life.

fried rice

wonton soup

Dragon Boat Festival

Lunar New Year

The Chinese celebrate holidays throughout the year. The first **new moon** brings the Lunar New Year, when people light firecrackers in the streets to scare away evil spirits. Chinese families also open their doors and windows. According to tradition, this allows the luck of the new year into their homes. The Dragon Boat Festival, or *Duanwu* Festival, takes place in spring. People sail boats on the lakes and rivers. They offer rice dumplings to the water. The Mid-Autumn Festival, or Moon Festival, happens in late summer. People enjoy a picnic at night under the moon.

National Day falls on October 1. This celebrates the founding of the People's Republic of China, which took place in 1949. On this day, people gather in public places to watch parades and listen to speeches.

The Great Wall

The Great Wall runs about 5,500 miles (8,850 kilometers) through northern China. First built over 2,000 years ago, it protected the Chinese kingdom against invaders from the north. The Great Wall winds through the countryside, over hills, and across the tops of mountains.

Some parts of the wall are disappearing. Stones from the wall have been taken to build new buildings. Other sections of the wall are falling apart because of **erosion**. The Chinese want to protect the wall and rebuild it. They want to keep this important piece of Chinese history and culture standing for future generations.

fun fact

Thousands of guards lived in the Great Wall's high towers. They kept watch over the countryside and rarely left their posts.

Did you know?
Today, marathons are held along the Great Wall. They are very difficult because runners have to go up and down thousands of steps!

27

Fast Facts About China

China's Flag

The flag of China has a red background. The red stands for the Chinese revolution of 1949. There are five yellow stars in the upper left corner. The large star stands for the Communist Party. The four smaller stars stand for the different Chinese people.

Official Name: People's Republic of China

Area: 3,705,407 square miles (9,596,961 square kilometers); China is the 4th largest country in the world.

Capital City:	Beijing
Important Cities:	Shanghai, Guangzhou, Tianjin
Population:	1,330,141,295 (July 2010)
Official Language:	Mandarin Chinese
National Holiday:	National Day (October 1)
Religions:	Daoism, Buddhism, Atheism, Christianity, Islam
Major Industries:	farming, fishing, manufacturing, mining, services
Natural Resources:	coal, iron ore, bauxite, salt, copper, manganese, oil, natural gas
Manufactured Products:	cars, ships, furniture, clothing, shoes, toys, electronics, sports equipment
Farm Products:	rice, millet, barley, wheat, tea, corn, peanuts, sweet potatoes, livestock
Unit of Money:	yuan

Glossary

badminton—a game played with racquets, a high net, and a small shuttlecock; players hit the shuttlecock back and forth over the net.

bamboo—a tall, thin plant that grows in China; bamboo is eaten by the Chinese people and giant pandas, and it is also used as a building material.

chopsticks—a pair of short, thin sticks that Chinese people use to eat food

dumplings—balls of dough filled with meat or vegetables

endangered—close to becoming extinct

erosion—the slow wearing away of something by water or wind

fertile—supports growth

forage—to look for food

herbs—plants used in cooking; most herbs are used to add flavor to food.

martial arts—styles and techniques of fighting and self-defense

natural resources—materials in the earth that are taken out and used to make products or fuel

new moon—the phase of the moon when it appears completely in shadow in the night sky

plateau—an area of flat, raised land

service jobs—jobs that perform tasks for people or businesses

To Learn More

AT THE LIBRARY
Dramer, Kim. *People's Republic of China*. New York, N.Y.: Children's Press, 2007.

Qing, Zheng. *China*. Hauppauge, N.Y.: Barron's Educational, 2006.

Salas, Laura Purdie. *China*. Mankato, Minn.: Bridgestone Books, 2002.

ON THE WEB
Learning more about China is as easy as 1, 2, 3.

1. Go to www.factsurfer.com.

2. Enter "China" into the search box.

3. Click the "Surf" button and you will see a list of related Web sites.

With factsurfer.com, finding more information is just a click away.

Index

The images in this book are reproduced through the courtesy of: Perkus, front cover; Maisei Raman, front cover (flag), p. 28; Jon Eppard, pp. 4-5; Zhu Difeng, pp. 6-7; Jamie Marshall/Tribaleye Images/Getty Images, p. 8; Alexey Shevelev, p. 9; Juan Martinez, pp. 9 (small), 11 (top), 23 (bottom), 24; Rosanne Tackaberry/Alamy, pp. 10-11; Stuart Berman, p. 11 (middle); Dean Bertoncelj, p. 11 (bottom); Philippe Michel/Age Fotostock, p. 12; Robert Francis/Photolibrary, p. 14; Bill Bachmann/Age Fotostock, p. 15; Mark Henley/Photolibrary, p. 16; Eddy Buttarelli/Getty Images, p. 17; Nancy Brown/Getty Images, p. 18; TAO Images Limited/Photolibrary, p. 19 (left); Becky Reed/Photolibrary, p. 19 (right); Christian Kober/Photolibrary, p. 20; GoGo Images/Photolibrary, p. 21; Jacob Halaska/Photolibrary, p. 22; Nayashkova Olga, p. 23 (top); Neil Farrin/Photolibrary, p. 25; Scott Truesdale, pp. 26-27, 29 (coin); Alain Even/Photolibrary, p. 26 (small); Black Rock Digital, p. 29 (bill).